WORLD IN
FOCUS

FOCUS ON
AUSTRALIA

OTTO JAMES

WORLD ALMANAC® LIBRARY

Please visit our web site at: www.garethstevens.com
For a free color catalog describing World Almanac® Library's list of high-quality books
and multimedia programs, call 1-800-848-2928 (USA) or 1-800-387-3178 (Canada).
World Almanac® Library's fax: (414) 332-3567.

Library of Congress Cataloging-in-Publication Data

James, Otto.
    Focus on Australia / Otto James. — North American ed.
      p. cm. — (World in focus)
    Includes bibliographical references and index.
    ISBN-13: 978-0-8368-6737-4 (lib. bdg.)
    ISBN-13: 978-0-8368-6744-2 (softcover)
    1. Australia—Juvenile literature. I. Title.
    DU96.J344   2007
    994—dc22   2006029358

This North American edition first published in 2007 by
World Almanac® Library
A Member of the WRC Media Family of Companies
330 West Olive Street, Suite 100
Milwaukee, WI 53212 USA

This U.S. edition copyright © 2007 by World Almanac® Library. Original edition
copyright © 2007 by Wayland. First published in 2007 by Wayland, an imprint
of Hachette Children's Books, 338 Euston Road, London NW1 3BH, U.K.

Commissioning editor: Nicola Edwards
Editor: Patience Coster
Inside design: Chris Halls, www.mindseyedesign.co.uk
Series concept and project management by EASI-Educational Resourcing
(info@easi-er.co.uk)
Statistical research: Anna Bowden
Maps and graphs: Martin Darlison, Encompass Graphics

World Almanac® Library editor: Alan Wachtel
World Almanac® Library cover design: Scott Krall

Picture acknowledgements. The author and publisher would like to thank the following for allowing their pictures to be reproduced
in this publication:
Chris Fairclough Worldwide/Chris Fairclough 14, 19, 31, 42, 55; Corbis cover top and 57 (Barry Lewis), 8 (Frans Lanting),
9 (Swim Ink 2, LLC), 10 (Historical Picture Archive), 12 (Bettmann), 13 (Bettmann), 17 (Jon Jones/Sygma), 22 (Paul A Souders),
23 (David Gray/Reuters), 24 (Will Burgess/Pool/epa), 26 (David Austen/zefa), 27 (David G Houser/Post-Houserstock),
30 (Paul A Souders), 33 (Tim Wimborne/Reuters), 34 (Hulton-Deutsch Collection), 36 (Reuters), 38 (William Caram),
41 (Mick Tsikas/epa), 45 (Robert Garvey), 46 (Reuters), 47 (Reuters), 48 (Alberto Estevez/epa), 49 (Duomo), 50 (Franz-Marc Frei),
58 (STR/epa); EASI-Images (Rob Bowden) cover bottom, 4, 5, title page and 15, 16, 18, 20, 25, 29, 32, 35, 39, 40, 43, 51, 52, 53, 54,
56, 59; EASI-Images (Dawne Fahey) 6, 21, 28, 37, 44; Topfoto 11 (HIP).

The directional arrow portrayed on the map on page 7 provides only an approximation of north.
The data used to produce the graphics and data panels in this title were the latest available at the time of production.

Printed in China

1 2 3 4 5 6 7 8 9 10 09 08 07 06

CONTENTS

Cover: The Sydney Opera House is one of Australia's most distinctive buildings.

Title page: Tourists admire the view from the edge of a steep cliff face in the Blue Mountains, in New South Wales.

CHAPTER 1

Australia –
An Overview

Australia occupies a giant island in the Southern Hemisphere, located between the South Pacific Ocean and the Indian Ocean. For tens of thousands of years this island was isolated from the rest of the world by the vast seas surrounding it. Australian plants and animals developed in their own, often distinctive, ways. The native Australians, known today as Indigenous Australian people, also developed their own unique way of life.

BRITISH SETTLERS

Australia only began to be settled by people from elsewhere in the world in the late-eighteenth century. In 1788, the first British settlers landed in a group of ships now known as the "First Fleet."

Until the twentieth century, Australia's different regions were separate; they did not become linked together as one country until 1901.

The population of Australia is relatively young compared to that of other developed nations. During the twentieth century, Australia's population grew rapidly, mainly as a result of the immigration of young people from other countries. Perhaps Australia's large number of young people is the reason why many people in the country have a youthful outlook on life.

▼ Sydney Harbor Bridge is one of Australia's most famous landmarks. This night view of Sydney also shows the Opera House on the left in the background.

▶ People on a busy shopping street near the Queen Victoria Building in Sydney. Many recent immigrants to Australia have come from Asia, especially from Southeast Asian countries such as Korea and Vietnam. Others have come from troubled regions such as Kosovo and Afghanistan.

WHERE PEOPLE LIVE

All the major settlements in Australia are coastal cities. The country's interior cannot support large numbers of people because it is mainly hot, arid desert that most people find too harsh of an environment in which to live. Nine out of every ten Australians live in cities or urban areas. This is more than in most other countries; in the year 2000, only 11 other countries had 90 percent of their people living in urban areas.

Australian cities—especially the largest ones such as Sydney and Melbourne—have become increasingly multicultural since the 1950s. Many of the most recent immigrants to Australia have come from Asia. Earlier immigrants included Europeans from Britain, Italy, Poland, Greece, and elsewhere in Europe, as well as people from Lebanon. In the less multicultural rural areas of Australia, most people are descended from British immigrants.

 Did You Know?

About 1,500 different kinds of fish live on the Great Barrier Reef.

Focus on: The Great Barrier Reef

Lying off the northeast coast of Australia is one of the wonders of the natural world: the Great Barrier Reef. The Great Barrier Reef is the largest coral reef in the world, stretching for more than 1,200 miles (2,000 kilometers). Diving or snorkeling trips to its shallow waters are one of Australia's most popular attractions. People come to see the variety of animals living there, from the tiny coral polyps of which the reef is composed to sea turtles and great white sharks.

▲ An abandoned tractor rusts on cattle-grazing land between the opal fields of Lightning Ridge and Sheepyard Mine in the Australian Outback of New South Wales.

INDIGENOUS AUSTRALIANS

Indigenous Australians are made up of two groups: Aborigines, who originally lived on the mainland, and Torres Strait Islanders, who originally came from the islands north of Australia. Wherever they live, whether in rural or urban areas, Indigenous Australians are generally worse off than other Australians because they miss out on the benefits of life in a modern, wealthy country. They tend to live in worse housing, do less well at school, miss out on job opportunities, and have shorter lives. They are Australia's poorest people and were not given the same rights as other Australians until the 1960s. In spite of this, some Indigenous Australians have become very successful and today number among high-profile judges, doctors, actors, and athletes.

THE OUTBACK

The image many people have in mind when they think of Australia is of the Outback, or the Red Center. In this area, red soils, blue skies, and sparse water supplies make for a beautiful but harsh environment. Amazing rock formations occasionally break up the flat landscape.

Much of Australia's early wealth depended on resources available in the Outback. Mineral wealth lies under the surface of many areas: gold, opals, iron, and other ores are mined and sold abroad. At the fringes of the Outback lie lands that can be used for agriculture. Although not generally suited to arable farming, this land is fine for keeping sheep, which can survive by grazing on the sparse vegetation. Parts of the Outback have giant sheep stations that produce wool and meat for export.

Physical Geography Data

- Land area: 2,940,521 sq miles/ 7,617,930 sq km

- Water area: 26,603 sq miles/68,920 sq km

- Total area: 2,967,124 sq miles/ 7,686,850 sq km

- World rank (by area): 6

- Land boundaries: 0 km/0 miles

- Border countries: None

- Coastline: 16,007 miles/25,760 km

- Highest point: Mount Kosciuszko (7,313 feet/2,229 m)

- Lowest point: Lake Eyre (-49 feet/-15 m)

Source: CIA World Factbook

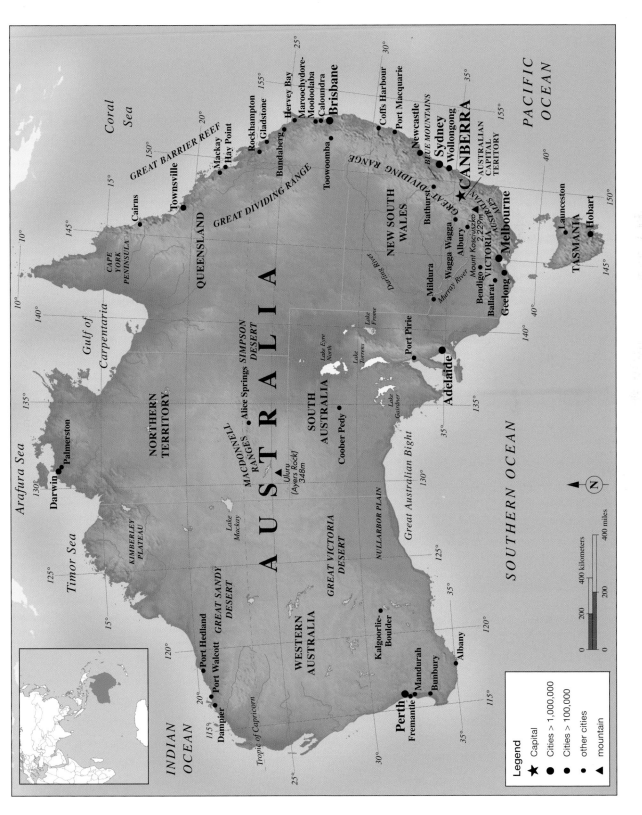

Coral Sea

PACIFIC OCEAN

GREAT BARRIER REEF

GREAT DIVIDING RANGE

Cairns

Townsville

Mackay
Hay Point

Rockhampton
Gladstone
Bundaberg
Hervey Bay
Maroochydore-
Mooloolaba
Caloundra
Brisbane

Toowoomba

Coffs Harbour
Port Macquarie
Newcastle
BLUE MOUNTAINS
Sydney
Wollongong
CANBERRA
AUSTRALIAN
CAPITAL
TERRITORY

QUEENSLAND

NEW SOUTH WALES

Bathurst
Wagga Wagga
Albury
Mount Kosciuszko
2,229m
Mildura
Bendigo
Ballarat
Geelong
Melbourne

Murray River
Darling River

Lake
Frome

VICTORIA

Launceston
Hobart
TASMANIA

CAPE YORK PENINSULA

Gulf of Carpentaria

Arafura Sea

Timor Sea

NORTHERN TERRITORY

Palmerston
Darwin

KIMBERLEY PLATEAU

Lake Mackay

SIMPSON DESERT

Alice Springs

MACDONNELL RANGES

Uluru
(Ayers Rock)
348m

A U S T R A L I A

SOUTH AUSTRALIA

Lake Eyre North

Lake Torrens

Lake Gairdner

Coober Pedy

Port Pirie

Port Augusta

Adelaide

Great Australian Bight

SOUTHERN OCEAN

GREAT SANDY DESERT

WESTERN AUSTRALIA

GREAT VICTORIA DESERT

NULLARBOR PLAIN

Port Hedland
Port Walcott
Dampier

Tropic of Capricorn

Kalgoorlie-Boulder

Albany

Mandurah
Bunbury

Perth
Fremantle

INDIAN OCEAN

N

0   200   400 kilometers
0   200   400 miles

Legend
★ Capital
● Cities > 1,000,000
● Cities > 100,000
· other cities
▲ mountain

CHAPTER 2

History

Australia's history dates back to when Indigenous Australians arrived on the continent from Asia. Some experts believe that their arrival was 65,000 years ago, while others think they arrived only 40,000 years ago. Either way, Indigenous Australians have been living in Australia for a long time.

LIVING WITH THE LAND

The Indigenous Australians settled across most of the continent, including in the interior. They developed a way of life that allowed them to cope with the harsh environment. Indigenous Australians lived in kinship groups, and, for thousands of years, their way of life continued without interruption from the outside world. During this time, the climate gradually became drier, wetter, and then drier again. Indigenous Australian populations shrank or grew as the climate changed. During the driest periods, there was not enough food and water for large numbers of people to survive, but during the wetter periods, more people were able to live off the land. By the time the First Fleet arrived in Australia in 1788, there were probably about 750,000 Indigenous Australian people living across the continent. It is often assumed that the Indigenous Australians lived only in the hot desert areas, but they also lived on the coasts and in the colder areas to the south. Tasmania, an island off Australia's south coast, had a large population of Indigenous Australians.

EUROPEAN EXPLORERS

Australia's name comes from the Latin word *australis*, which means "southern." For centuries, Europeans had spoken of *Terra Australis Incognita*—the Unknown Southern Land—but there was no proof that this mythical place existed. Then, in 1606, a Dutch navigator named Willem Jansz sighted Cape York Peninsula. This peninsula is located in the far northeast of Australia, in what is now the state of Queensland.

◄ Aboriginal artist Turkey Tolson Tjupurrula at work in the Central Desert in Australia's Northern Territory. Many Indigenous Australian artists use a style of painting that has been handed down through generations.

THE LANDING OF CAPTAIN COOK AT BOTANY BAY 1770

AUSTRALIA

▶ Captain Cook's arrival at Botany Bay is depicted in this poster from the 1930s promoting tourism in Australia.

Between 1616 and 1636, Dutch navigators explored Australia's west, southwest, and northwest coasts but did not try to settle in the land they called New Holland. In 1770, Captain James Cook of the British navy sighted and explored the fertile east coast of Australia. He claimed the region for Britain and called it New South Wales. This began Britain's acquisition of the whole continent.

"TRANSPORTATION"

In 1787, to relieve the overcrowding in its prisons, Britain began shipping convicts to prison colonies in New South Wales in a practice known as "transportation." In 1788, eleven ships carrying about 730 convicts—the First Fleet— arrived in Botany Bay, on Australia's east coast. Members of the fleet established a base about 7 miles (11 km) north of Botany Bay. This base eventually became the city of Sydney.

 Did You Know?

The boomerang is a traditional Indigenous Australian hunting weapon.

Focus on: Indigenous Australians

In 1788, there were roughly 500 different Indigenous Australian groups, each speaking its own language and each with strong ties to a particular area of land. Many Indigenous Australian myths and religious beliefs were linked to the land on which the people lived, with stories about almost every rock, stream, path, or other feature of the landscape. Each group was made up of small bands of people whose home was in a particular area. These bands rarely left their area, because trespassing on another band's territory could result in violence.

During the 1790s, the British colonial government allowed military officers and freed convicts to begin settling their own lands. Free immigrants also began to arrive from Britain. Other colonial settlements followed, including Tasmania, in 1803; Western Australia, in 1829; South Australia, in 1836; Victoria, in 1851; and Queensland, in 1859. The Northern Territory was established as a part of South Australia in 1863. In 1868, the British government finally abolished the practice of transportation.

EUROPEANS AND INDIGENOUS AUSTRALIANS

The arrival of Europeans was a disaster for Indigenous Australians across Australia. The settlers brought diseases, such as influenza and smallpox, to which the Indigenous Australians had no resistance, and many died as a result. Others were expelled from the land their people had occupied for thousands of years. Some Indigenous Australian leaders resisted the European settlers. In the late 1700s and early 1800s, warriors such as Pemulwy, Dundalli, and Jandamarra (also known as Pigeon) tried to fight the European invasion of their lands. But there was little they could do to stop the ever-increasing numbers of settlers. By the mid-1800s, the European settlers had erased all traces of the traditional Indigenous Australian lifestyle from Tasmania.

THE WOOL TRADE

During the 1820s, settlers in New South Wales started to export wool back to Britain. This lucrative trade formed the basis for a strong economy, and increasing numbers of settlers decided to become sheep farmers. During the 1830s, some farmers moved from Tasmania and the area around Sydney to the rich grazing lands in southern New South Wales. There, they founded the city of Melbourne. These settlers asked the British government for permission to become a separate colony. In 1851, the area south of the Murray River became known as the colony of Victoria.

◄ This Gold Rush prospector was photographed in Queensland in 1867. The Gold Rush brought new citizens to Australia. Some of these people stayed in Australia because they failed to find gold and could not afford the trip home.

In 1851, gold was found in New South Wales and Victoria. Thousands of people from overseas rushed to Australia to make their fortunes. Some became very rich, but others did not make enough money to pay for their journeys home. They remained in Australia, swelling the non-Indigenous population from 400,000 in 1850 to 1,100,000 in 1860.

During the 1850s, most of the Australian colonies had been granted self-government.

But, by the 1890s, a growing number of Australians had begun to think that the separate colonies would be better off as a single nation. Among other benefits, forming a single nation would mean that Britain would no longer be able to tax goods crossing Australia's internal borders. In 1897 and 1898, a constitution was drawn up, and, on January 1, 1901, the colonies finally became united in a federation of states known as the Commonwealth of Australia.

Focus on: Expedition to the Interior

The first European settlers to explore Australia's interior became great celebrities. In 1860, Robert Burke and William Wills led an expedition with the plan to cross Australia from south to north. They set out with a two-year supply of food. Burke and Wills, plus two other men named John King and Charles Gray, reached Australia's north coast in 1861, but only one man would survive the return journey. Gray died on the way back. Burke, Wills, and King reached one of their old camps and waited there for supplies. The two leaders starved to death. The sole survivor was King, who was rescued by Indigenous Australians.

▼ An illustration of the Burke and Wills expedition setting out from Melbourne on August 20, 1860.

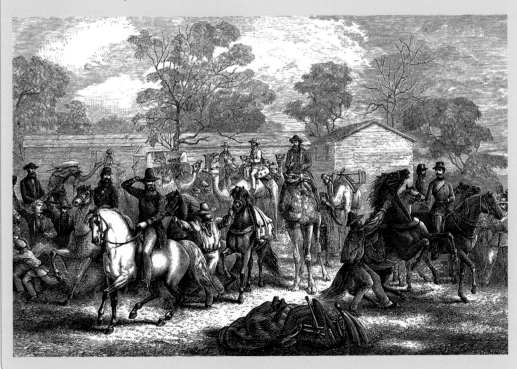

TWENTIETH-CENTURY AUSTRALIA

Although Australia had become a single nation by 1901, it kept close ties with Britain, and the British monarch remained Australia's head of state. Australia supported Britain in wars and conflicts, and Australian armed forces were involved in fighting in the Boer War (1899–1902) in South Africa. More than 400,000 Australian troops also served in Europe on the side of Britain in World War I (1914–1918).

THE "WHITE AUSTRALIA POLICY"

Soon after becoming a federation, Australia passed the Immigration Restriction Bill. This was the start of what became known unofficially as the "White Australia policy," which aimed to prevent immigration by nonwhite, non-European people. For many decades, most new Australians came from Europe. Some of the country's key immigration restrictions were not abolished until 1958, and its racially based immigration practices lasted until 1973. While discouraging nonwhite immigration, Australia was trying to attract immigrants from Europe. British people, for example, were encouraged to start a "New Life Down Under"—"down under" meaning on the other side of the world—by cheap travel and relocation costs. After World War II, immigration increased Australia's population significantly and helped to create a period of increasing wealth.

During World War II (1939–1945), Robert Menzies was prime minister of Australia. He held the office again between 1949 and 1966 and oversaw a period of prosperity for many people. Menzies kept close ties with Britain and is Australia's longest-serving prime minister.

▼ A photographer takes pictures as Australian troops land on the coast of Borneo in 1945.

WARS ABROAD

During World War I, young Australian men went to Europe to fight for Britain. Many of these "Diggers," as they are called, lost their lives at battles such as Gallipoli, where one-third of the Australian soldiers there died and two-thirds were wounded. During World War II, many Australian soldiers went to Europe and North Africa to fight. They returned home to defend Australia and fight the Japanese after Japan entered the war in 1941. This "War in the Pacific" created close links with the United States, which proved to be a more useful ally than distant Britain. Australia's involvement in conflict in Asia continued with U.S.-led wars against communist forces in Korea (1950–1953) and Vietnam (1957–1975).

In 1964, Australia introduced conscription, and many young Australian men were sent to fight in Vietnam. The Vietnam War and the conscription that accompanied it were a turning point for Australia. Many Australians objected to young men being sent to fight in a war they did not support, and protests followed.

A CHANGE OF GOVERNMENT

Public disapproval of Australia's involvement in the Vietnam War contributed toward the election of a new government in 1972. The new prime minister, Gough Whitlam, made far-reaching changes. His government withdrew troops from Vietnam, abolished conscription, introduced free national health care, and supported Indigenous Australians in their attempts to regain some of the land they had once occupied. Whitlam also presided over a period of high unemployment and inflation.

▶ Demonstrators protest the Vietnam War in Sydney in 1966.

In 1975, Whitlam was fired as prime minister by the governor general, the unelected representative of the British crown in Australia. This action sowed the seeds of a controversy that continues today: Should Australia free itself of its ties with Britain and become a republic, or should it remain a constitutional monarchy?

During the 1980s, Australia became more open to immigration from Asia. Some of the new immigrants were people from Korea and Vietnam, whose parents' generation had seen Australian troops fighting in their countries.

CHAPTER 3

Landscape and Climate

▲ Salt lakes such as this one, which is relatively small, form in Australia's driest inland regions.

Australia is one of the oldest landmasses on Earth. Parts of its western area, called the Australian Craton, are 3.8 billion years old. Its eastern area, the Tasman Fold Belt, is far younger, at 250–500 million years old. The whole continent is slowly drifting northward, at just 2.2 inches (55 millimeters) a year.

Lying beneath about 20 percent of Australia is one of the world's largest groundwater stores, the Great Artesian Basin. The Outback of eastern Australia depends on the Basin for its water supplies.

HILLS, DESERTS, AND SALT LAKES

Australia's east coast has a narrow, fertile strip of land at the Pacific Ocean's edge. Behind this, the land rises up into the Great Dividing

Range, a line of hills that stretches from north to south across almost the whole continent. The Great Dividing Range is not particularly high in most places; even Mount Kosciuszko, Australia's highest mountain, is just 7,313 feet (2,229 m), less than half the height of Mont Blanc in France and just over one-third as high as Mount McKinley in the United States.

West of the Great Dividing Range, Australia's landscape gradually becomes the flat and dry Outback. This interior landscape is mainly one of barren semideserts and dry salt lakes mixed with some areas that are able to support sheep and other livestock farms. The flatness of the landscape is broken only by rock formations such as Uluru and Kata Tjuta (the Olgas). There are also a few mountainous areas, such as the MacDonnell Ranges, located in the center of Australia, near Alice Springs.

Western Australia is made up mainly of a broad plateau. The southern strip of the west coast has a fertile area beside the Indian Ocean. Farther north, the Outback extends as far as the sea.

Australia divides into four basic climatic zones: tropical, mostly in northern areas; desert, mostly in the Outback; semitropical, mainly in south-eastern areas; and temperate, mainly in the south.

 Did You Know?

Some Australian rocks contain crystals dating from 3.8 billion years ago. They are so old that they were once part of Earth's original crust.

▶ This famous viewpoint looks out over the edge of a steep cliff face in the Blue Mountains. It is visited by thousands of people each month.

Focus on: Uluru and Kata Tjuta

Uluru, or Ayers Rock, is a rock formation that soars up out of the flat desert lands in the Australian Outback. It is 2.2 miles (3.6 km) long and 1,142 feet (348 meters) high. About two-thirds of the rock is hidden beneath the sandy soil that makes up the surrounding land. Uluru attracts visitors who are eager to see the way the rock changes color from deep ocher at sunrise and sunset to brighter reds as the sun climbs higher in the sky. About nineteen miles (30 kilometers) west of Uluru is another mysterious rock formation, Kata Tjuta. This is a collection of smaller, rounder rocks. Its name means "many heads" in the local Aboriginal language.

RAINFALL AND DROUGHT

Northern Australia is sometimes called "the Top End" and has a climate distinct from the rest of the country. This region is tropical, with most of its rainfall concentrated into a short season. Parts of the northeast coast of Queensland can receive as much as 150 inches (380 centimeters) of rain a year, compared to the 10–20 inches (25-50 cm) received by most of the rest of the country. This is where Australia's remaining areas of rain forest are located.

The Top End has only a wet season, from November to April, and a dry season. The wet season can bring violent storms, known as cyclones. In 1974, the coastal town of Darwin was almost flattened by a cyclone.

A less extreme wet season brings rainfall to Australia's southeast and far southwest coasts. The dry seasons of these regions can be very dry, and droughts frequently occur even in areas with reasonable annual rainfall. One problem caused by droughts is forest fires. These fires happen during the dry season, when the vegetation has lost its moisture and easily catches fire. Forest fires have always been a part of Australia's ecosystem. Most of the country's trees and plants have adapted to survive them. Some have developed fire-resistant seeds. In recent years, however, increasing numbers of people have built homes in the country's scrubby forested areas, or "bush," on the high ground of the coastal inland areas. These homes can easily be destroyed if a fire springs up nearby.

The Outback is the driest region of Australia, with many areas receiving less than 10 inches (25 cm) of rain each year. Its soils are thin and only a few types of tough plants can grow in it.

TEMPERATURES

The tropical northern region of Australia has warm or hot temperatures all year. The town of Cairns, for example, has permanent temperatures of 68–86 °Fahrenheit (20–30 °Celsius), which means that people wear shorts and T-shirts all year round. The same is not true of the far south. In Tasmania, the city of Hobart's average temperatures range between 41 °F and 68 °F (5 °C and 20 °C). In winter, temperatures can fall below freezing for several days in a row. Similar temperatures occur in Melbourne, on the mainland. Many of the

◄ The temperate rain forests of New South Wales and Queensland are a popular attraction. Some of the money visitors spend in these areas is used to help conserve the rain forests.

country's coastal cities, however, have temperatures somewhere between these two extremes, with warm weather for much of the year.

The Australian Outback sees the widest variations of temperature. During summers, daytime temperatures in the Outback regularly exceed 104 °F (40 °C) , while the thermometer often drops below freezing at night. The Outback's hottest months are during Australia's summer, which lasts from October to March.

? Did You Know?

Australia's southern Alps are covered in snow in winter. They are the only place on the continent where people can go skiing.

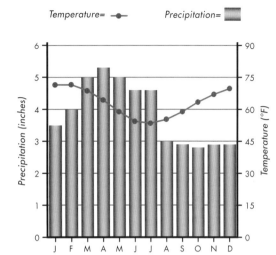

Temperature= ●   Precipitation= ▮

▲ Average monthly climate conditions in Sydney

▼ A firefighter radios for help as a forest fire blazes out of control in the bush outside Sydney.

CHAPTER 4

Population and Settlements

Although Australia is about the same size as the mainland of the United States, the country has only about 20 million people, compared to the 290 million people living in the United States. This suggests that Australians live surrounded by plenty of open space. In a sense, this is true—there are large, empty spaces all over Australia. But many parts of the country are not suitable for people to live in. Lack of water and other resources, together with the hot, dry climate, mean that large areas of the Outback can only support a small population. Most Australians inhabit cities or towns and live close to other people.

CITIES AND SUBURBS

Since 1950, Australia's population has grown, and an increasing number of Australians have started to live in cities. In 1950, 75.1 percent of Australians lived in an urban environment. By 2005, that figure had reached 92 percent. The city centers of Sydney, Melbourne, and Perth, for example, are home to a large relatively young population, although older people also live in

Did You Know?

Forecasts predict that by 2030, 96 percent of Australians will live in cities and towns.

them. Clubs, restaurants, bars, and sports venues cater to city-living Australians. The inner cities are becoming increasingly popular places to live. Most Australians, however, live in suburbs. These are urban areas outside the city centers. As the urban population has grown, so too has the area covered by the suburbs. In Sydney, for example, the western suburbs now stretch out to the Blue Mountains, which form a barrier to further suburban expansion. These suburbs are over an hour's journey from the city center.

◀ This picture of a busy street in Sydney shows the rail that carries the monorail train around the city center (*center top*).

▲ Suburban houses like these tend to be a long way from shops and other facilities, which is one reason why Australians often use their cars to get around.

Many Australians depend on their cars to travel long distances to work every day from the sprawling suburbs. Typical homes in Australia's suburbs are bigger than those in the city centers. Many of them are detached houses with large gardens and, sometimes, a swimming pool.

RICH AND POOR

Australia's various suburbs are very different in character. Sydney's northern beaches, for example, are home to some of the most glamorous properties in the country, including ultramodern steel and glass villas that overlook beautiful stretches of sea and shore. At the other extreme are the suburban areas that have traditionally been home to poorly paid workers and new immigrants. Most of these areas are inland and far from the city centers.

NEW IMMIGRANTS

Much of the growth in Australia's population during the twentieth century was the result of immigration. Initially, immigrants to Australia tended to come from Europe. In 1901, almost 80 percent of immigrant Australians were from

Population Data

- Population: 20.2 million
- Population 0–14 yrs: 20%
- Population 15–64 yrs: 68%
- Population 65+ yrs: 12%
- Population growth rate: 1.1%
- Population density: 6.8 per sq mile/ 2.6 per sq km
- Urban population: 92%
- Major cities: Sydney 4,388,000, Melbourne 3,663,000, Brisbane 1,769,000, Perth 1,484,000, Adelaide 1,137,000

Source: United Nations and World Bank

Britain. Later in the century, a smaller proportion of immigrants were from Britain, and, by 1954, the figure was just 52 percent. Also in 1954, 33 percent of European immigrants to Australia were from Italy, Greece, Germany, the Netherlands, and Poland.

During the 1980s and 1990s, after the abolition of racially based immigration laws, immigrants to Australia began to arrive from Southeast Asia and the Indian subcontinent. By 2002, 15 percent

of immigrant Australians were from Asian or Pacific countries such as China, Vietnam, the Philippines, India, Malaysia, and Sri Lanka. In 1954, people from these countries made up just 2 percent of immigrant Australians.

New immigrants to Australia typically live in major cities, where they are more likely to find work and come across other people who speak their native language and are familiar with their culture. This means that rural areas have not received as many immigrants as Australian towns and cities. As a result, the government of Australia now makes it easier for people to immigrate to the country if they are willing to spend time working in rural areas.

SHRINKING RURAL POPULATIONS

Most of Australia's rural towns grew up as focal points for their local economies. In agricultural areas, they were places where farmers could bring their goods to market and for transportation to the big cities. Other rural towns grew up around different industries, such as mining.

As long as the mines stay open—and mining is one of Australia's biggest industries— rural mining towns have tended to survive and

 Did You Know?

The world's largest cattle farm is at Anna Creek, Australia. It covers 13,124 sq miles (34,000 sq km)—an area larger than Belgium.

◀ Sydney's Chinatown district. Since the 1980s, increasing numbers of Chinese people have immigrated to Australia. Many of the country's recent immigrants have come from elsewhere in Asia.

even thrive. The same cannot be said of some towns in farming areas. The increase in long-distance travel; the effect of the Internet upon rural businesses, which now have to compete with far-away shops in the cities, and lose customers as a result; and the lure of the facilities in bigger cities have stripped many rural towns of their businesses and young people.

Since 1950, Australia's rural population has shrunk at a rate of up to 4 percent every five years. In 1950, there were slightly more than 2 million Australians living in the country's rural areas. By 2000, the country's rural population had dropped to 1.8 million, and it is forecast that this segment of the population will be fewer than 1 million by 2030. At the same time, the country's overall population has increased, meaning that a smaller and smaller proportion of Australians live in rural areas.

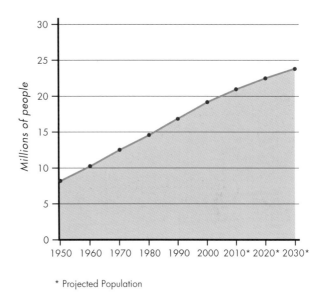

* Projected Population

▲ Population growth, 1950–2030

▼ Greek-Australian dancers perform a traditional Greek dance at a festival in Gosford, which is located in New South Wales.

CHAPTER 5

Government and Politics

Australia is a federal state, which means that it has a central government but its different territories have the power to control some of their own affairs. The country's main political parties are the Australian Labor Party and the Liberal Party. Other smaller parties include the National Country Party and the Australian Democrats.

FEDERAL GOVERNMENT

Australia's federal government controls the country's economy, taxes, immigration, defense, and foreign policy. The federal government is based in Canberra, which has its own territory, the Australian Capital Territory (ACT). The ACT, which surrounds the city, makes Canberra independent of Australia's other states, because it is not a part of any of them.

One reason for ACT's existence is the rivalry that exists between Australia's states—especially between Victoria and New South Wales. If Sydney, which is located in New South Wales, had become the country's capital city, the people of Victoria would have been unhappy. If Melbourne, located in Victoria, had been chosen, the people of New South Wales would have been unhappy. In the end, a whole new city was built, with a new territory around it.

No Australian government is allowed to remain in office for more than three years without an election being held. Usually the prime minister, the leader of the government, chooses to call an election before the three year term is up.

▼ Tourists view the Australian National Parliament House from the summit of Mount Ainslie in Canberra.

▶ Prime Minister John Howard holds a Bible as his Liberal Party government is sworn-in in Canberra on October 26, 2004.

The government is made up of two parts, the House of Representatives and the Senate. The House of Representatives has 148 members. Each of Australia's 6 states and 2 territories elects a number of representatives based on its population, which means that the states with the biggest populations get the most representatives. In 2006, New South Wales had 50 representatives, Victoria had 37, Queensland had 27, South Australia had 12, Western Australia had 14, Tasmania had 5, ACT had 2, and the Northern Territory had 1. The political party with the most seats in the House of Representatives chooses the ministers who will run the country, including the prime minister.

Australia's second governing body is the Senate. The Senate has 12 senators from each of the 6 states and 2 from each of the territories. The Senate can block legislation from the House of Representatives, balancing power between the large and small states.

 Did You Know?

Voting in elections is compulsory in Australia. In spite of this, prosecutions for failure to vote are rare and fines are nominal.

Focus on: Canberra

Canberra is one of the few cities in the world that did not grow up from a smaller settlement. Instead, in 1912, American architect Walter Burley Griffin won an international competition to design it from scratch. Canberra's name was taken from an Aboriginal word thought to mean "meeting place." Canberra is halfway between Sydney and Melbourne, and it is the only major city in Australia that is not on the country's coast. Australia's parliament first met there in 1927, although the city was not really finished until after World War II.

STATE GOVERNMENTS

Australia's state governments are led by a premier or, in Northern Territory, a chief minister. The difference between the two is in name only. Australia's state governments have the same structure as the federal government, with two governing bodies, although Queensland abolished its Senate in 1922.

The main responsibilities of the country's state governments are health, education, housing, transportation, and local law enforcement. Most taxes are raised by the federal government, which then releases some of this money to the states. The money from the federal government is rarely enough for major new projects, such as large sports facilities or new roads. Money for these projects is raised through extra payments or loans, usually from the federal government.

This means that Australia's federal government has a lot of control over the state governments.

LOCAL GOVERNMENTS

Within each state in Australia, there is a third layer of government, made up mainly of shire, town, or city councils. Shires are small rural regions. These governments maintain and build local roads, make sure garbage is collected, fund local libraries, and perform other similar day-to-day tasks. Local governments in Australia, like state governments, are mainly financed by the federal government.

▼Queen Elizabeth II of Britain plants a gum tree on the grounds of Government House in Canberra during the course of a five-day official visit to Australia in March 2006. She is watched by gardener Norm Dunn (*left*) and Prince Philip (*right*).

Focus on: Republicanism

Australia's head of state is the British monarch. For a long time, some Australians have wanted their country to become a republic and cut its ties with the British monarchy. This idea dates back hundreds of years. Irish people were among Australia's earliest settlers, and they arrived in the country with no love of the British monarchy. The debate over whether Australia should become a republic came to a head during the early 1990s, when Paul Keating was the country's prime minister. Keating was a republican who thought Australia should sever its ties with the "old country"—a term that was increasingly irrelevant to immigrant Australians who had no ties to Britain. Australia held a referendum in 1999 to decide the question. Almost every state rejected the proposal to become a republic, and Australia kept its ties with Britain.

CITIES AND STATES

In some of Australia's big cities, local government is divided among several areas of the city. This prevents a big city from becoming too powerful within a state. Sydney, for example, has 39 separate local government regions. This is partly because most of the people in New South Wales live within the area of Greater Sydney. If the people of Sydney were to elect their own mayor (which they do not at the moment), the result could be that more people voted for the mayor of Sydney than supported the premier of New South Wales. This could put the lower-ranking mayor of Sydney in a more powerful position than the higher-ranking state premier.

 Did You Know?

In the national referendum of 1999, only the Australian Capital Territory voted in favor of the country becoming a republic.

► The exterior of New South Wales's state parliament building, in Sydney.

CHAPTER 6

Energy and Resources

Most of Australia's energy—including 91.6 percent of its electricity—comes from fossil fuels, such as oil, coal, and natural gas. Of the rest, the bulk comes from hydroelectric power (HEP), which provides 7.2 percent of the country's electricity. Australia is the world's fourth biggest producer and its biggest exporter of coal. It also has large natural gas reserves, producing 8 percent of the world's supply. Natural gas production in Australia is projected to more than double between 1980 and 2020.

Australia does not have access to large amounts of its own oil, although there are reserves off the coast of Victoria, in South Australia, and in Western Australia. The country's known commercial oil reserves will probably be used up by 2015, compared to 2065 for natural gas and 2105 for coal. More energy resources may be found, and geologists have identified offshore regions where such discoveries may be made. In spite of this, Australia now has to import oil. Importing oil drains Australia's economy because the country has to buy oil from abroad instead of providing its own.

ENERGY CONSUMPTION

Australia uses a lot of energy, even compared to other wealthy nations. In 2000, each Australian used the equivalent of 6.9 tons (6.2 metric tons) of oil compared with Britain's 4.3 tons (3.9 metric tons) per person and Mexico's 1.7 tons (1.6 metric tons) per person. Higher users of energy include the United States at 9.2 tons (8.4 metric tons) per person.

There are various reasons for Australia's high energy use. The first is Australians' dependence on their cars. This is linked to the size of the country where, outside the city centers, walking or cycling is not always practical. Also, some big Australian industries, such as mining, metal production, and ore extraction, are typically large consumers of energy. A further reason

◀ This terrifying looking machine is a cutting machine for strip-mining coal.

that Australia uses a great deal of energy is the country's hot climate, which makes energy-hungry appliances like air-conditioners common in some areas.

ALTERNATIVE ENERGIES

Apart from hydroelectric power (HEP), Australia gets little of its energy from alternative sources. Given the country's long hours of sunshine, solar power offers abundant opportunities for this to change in the future. Australia's government is committed to trying to increase the use of alternative energies through hydro-electric, solar, biomass, and wind power.

NUCLEAR POWER

Although Australia is a major exporter of nuclear-power-grade uranium, it does not produce any of its own energy using nuclear power stations. The country's abundant supplies of cheap coal have in the past made nuclear power unnecessary.

▲ Parabolic solar energy dishes at a power station operated by the Solar Research Corporation of Melbourne.

 Did You Know?

Skiing became popular in Australia after 1949, when European hydroelectric workers on the Snowy Mountains power program practiced the sport. It is now a favorite winter pastime.

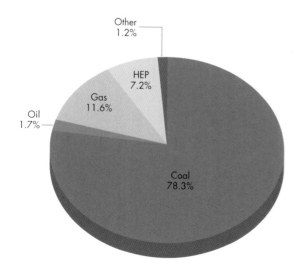

▲ Electricity production by type

Energy Data

📂 Energy consumption as % of world total: 1.1%

📂 Energy consumption by sector (% of total)

    Industry: 34.6

    Transportation: 39.2

    Agriculture: 2.3

    Services: 7.0

    Residential: 12.6

    Other: 4.3

📂 CO_2 emissions as % of world total: 1.4

📂 CO_2 emissions per capita in tons per year: 19.1

Source: World Resources Institute

▲ A miner drills in the opal fields near Lightning Ridge, in New South Wales.

MINERAL RESOURCES

Australia is rich in mineral resources. During the 1800s, reserves of copper, gold, silver, lead, tin, and zinc were discovered in the country. Deposits of diamonds were also found, as were the world's biggest deposits of high-quality opals. During the 1950s, geologists found huge deposits of iron ore, coal, and bauxite (the main source of aluminum).

Western Australia, Queensland, and New South Wales are the country's top mining states. Western Australia has large reserves of nickel, iron ore, gold, and bauxite. Copper, silver, and bauxite are found in Queensland. Coal, lead, and zinc are found in New South Wales. Australia is thought to have the world's largest undeveloped deposits of uranium in the Northern Territory and South Australia.

These mineral resources are often found in the least hospitable parts of the country, which means that the people who work them often live in isolated settlements. Roads and railways need to be built to reach new mines, making it expensive to develop new mining areas. Even with these obstacles, Australia is one of the world's leading miners of mineral resources.

AGRICULTURAL RESOURCES

While one-third of Australia's land is desert, farmland covers about 60 percent of the country. Only 10 percent of it, however, is suitable for crop growing. Most of the country's best soil is in its coastal areas. The rest of its farmland is mainly pastureland for animals such as sheep and cattle.

In the north, special crops—including tropical fruits, such as mangoes, and flowers, such as orchids—can be grown. Farther south, crops more associated with temperate climates are common. In this region, fruits such as apples,

Focus on: Coober Pedy

The town of Coober Pedy in South Australia advertises itself as "the Opal Capital of the World." It grew up around a cluster of opal mines, and its name is said to be a version of the Indigenous Australian words *kupa piti,* which mean "white man in a hole." Today, the town still supplies almost all the world's high-grade opal gemstones, but it has also become an unlikely tourist attraction. People come to visit the mines and see the unique underground lifestyle of the town. In the past, the baking desert heat drove some of the townspeople to live underground, where their homes (called "dugouts" by locals) stayed cool during the hot days.

together with sugar, wheat, potatoes, rice, and grapes for winemaking, are grown.

Australia's fishing resources are limited. Thousands of different kinds of fish live in the waters off Australia, but few edible species are present in large numbers. Australia's biggest fishing resources are shellfish such as abalones, lobsters, oysters, shrimp, and scallops.

The cooler southern regions of Australia have large forested areas where commercial quantities of wood can be harvested. Tasmania, in particular, has large areas of old-growth forest, which provide a major natural resource. Tasmania's trees include the rare huon pines, which are said to be the best wood for boat-building. However, logging in these forests is highly controversial because it has generally not been carried out in a sustainable way. Opponents claim that the logging industry is doing irreparable harm to the environment and animals, including many endangered species.

 Did You Know?

Australia produces nearly all its own food.

▼ These workers are picking grapes at a vineyard in the Hunter Valley, located east of Sydney. Wine is a relatively recent but very valuable export product for Australia.

CHAPTER 7

Economy and Income

Australia is a wealthy country, and its people enjoy a high standard of living. The country ranked twenty-fourth in the world by per person Gross National Income (GNI) in 2004–2005—slightly higher than Hong Kong, Italy, and Spain.

MINING AND AGRICULTURE

Australia's natural and mineral resources are important to its economy. Australia's wealth was built on the twin foundations of agriculture and mining, and these remain a vital part of its economy today. They are particularly important for exports. The products of agriculture and mining together make up roughly 65 percent of all of Australia's exported goods.

Mining and agriculture (including fishing and forestry) each contribute similar amounts to the country's economy. Mining contributes 4.9 percent, and agriculture contributes 3 percent. They also support the manufacturing industries, such as metal production or food and animal processing. The iron-ore mines, for example, produce ore that supplies Australia's important metal-processing industry. The manufacturing industries contribute an additional 15 percent to the country's economy.

Mining and agriculture also contribute to the wholesale and retail trades, which sell goods such as sheet metal, meat, and vegetables. While many of the goods sold by these trades are produced outside Australia, a proportion of the 10 percent contributed to the economy by this sector is derived from goods that are produced within Australia.

▼ A fisherman unloads and sorts a catch of sardines at the wharf in Lakes Entrance, in Victoria.

Many of Australia's agricultural businesses are based on animal husbandry, particularly cattle and sheep farming. Live animals and processed meat are produced for the home market and for export. Animal products such as wool also provide income. Grain is produced for the home market, and it is also an important export.

Australia's valuable mineral exports include metals, coal, and natural gas. Most of the country's mineral resources, such as its vast uranium deposits, remain untapped. This means that mining will play an important part in Australia's economy in the future.

FOREIGN OWNERSHIP
In the past, Australia lacked capital, or money to invest in developing new businesses. This made it difficult for the country to develop its economy. It meant that many businesses had to borrow capital from abroad. As a result, many of Australia's mining companies, factories, processing plants, and other businesses are owned by companies from Britain, the United States, or Japan. Australia's government recently passed a law declaring that at least

50 percent of new mining projects had to be Australian owned. Because of continuing lack of capital, however, this requirement is not always enforced.

▼ At the port of Adelaide, sheep are loaded onto a ship for export to the Middle East.

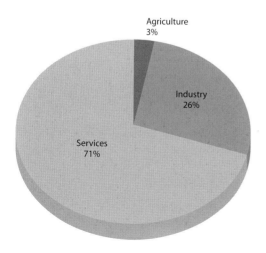

Agriculture 3%

Industry 26%

Services 71%

▲ Contribution by sector to national income

Economic Data

▢ Gross National Income (GNI) in U.S.$: 541,173,481,472
▢ World rank by GNI: 14
▢ GNI per capita in U.S.$: 26,900
▢ World rank by GNI per capita: 24
▢ Economic growth: 3.0%

Source: World Bank

SERVICE INDUSTRIES

Although Australia's wealth traditionally came from mining and agriculture, its economy is now dominated by its service industry. Taken together, in 2005, service industries contributed 71 percent of Australia's Gross Domestic Product (GDP)—up 9 percent from 2002.

The largest sector of Australia's service industry consists of its banking, financial, and property services, which contribute 17.5 percent of its GDP. Other important service industries include retail and wholesale trade (10.2 percent of GDP); transportation and communications (7.7 percent); and construction (6.3 per cent).

▼ The office of the Macquarie Bank in Sydney resembles bank offices found in developed countries around the world.

The fastest growth in the Australia's service sector has been in communications businesses, which provide telephone and e-mail services. The communications industry has recently averaged a growth rate of 6.4 percent. The country's most unstable business is construction. During the 1990s and early 2000s, Australia experienced a boom in the cost of housing, especially in the big cities, and this fueled growth in the construction industry. The boom in house prices has ended, however, and the people working in construction are now vulnerable to the threat of unemployment.

TOURISM

Tourism, which was substantially boosted when Sydney hosted the 2000 Olympic Games, makes an important contribution to Australia's

economy. Tourists spend substantial amounts of money in a variety of the country's service industries, including the travel, retail, hotel, and restaurant businesses.

Almost one-half of the tourist dollars spent in Australia is spent outside the major cities, so tourism is important to both the country's rural economy and its urban economy. In 2003–2004, more than half a million Australians worked in the tourist industry, which brought AUS$7.6 billion to the country's coffers. Total spending by international visitors was AUS$17.3 billion.

▲ Tourists watch the sun setting on Uluru (Ayers Rock). The site is a major Australian landmark. It attracts about 400,000 visitors every year.

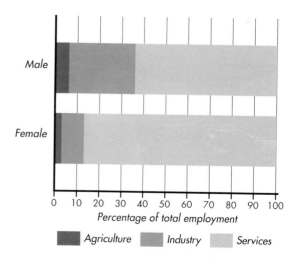

▲ Labor force by sector and gender

Did You Know?

Australian women earn almost one-third less than Australian men.

CHAPTER 8

Global Connections

In the past, Australia's main foreign links were with the West, especially with Britain and, later, with the United States. Even after Australia was united as a federation in 1901, it retained close links with Britain and tended to follow its lead in matters of foreign policy. This was shown by its decision to join the fight in Europe during World War I. The families of many Australians had originally come from Britain, and Australia still believed and trusted in its strong connection with "the old country." When Britain declared war on Germany in 1939, Australian prime minister Robert Menzies said: "There can be no doubt that where Great Britain stands, there stand the people of the entire British world." As a result, Australia entered World War II in 1939.

During World War II, Australia faced the possibility of an invasion by forces from Japan, which was then an ally of Germany. Between 1942 and 1943, Japanese aircraft bombed northern Australian targets a total of 93 times and killed hundreds of people. By this time, Britain's involvement in the war in Europe since 1939 had weakened it, and it was unable or unwilling to send help. Australia found instead that it had common interests with the United States, which was also fighting Japan in the Pacific region. The two countries worked together closely. By 1942, the U.S. Army's Pacific headquarters was based in Australia, and more than 120,000 U.S. troops were stationed there.

THE COLD WAR

As the twentieth century progressed, Australia's links with the United States became more important. Australia was a strong ally of the United States in its fight against communism in Asia during the Cold War. During the 1950s, Australia joined two international groups led by the United States. ANZUS linked Australia,

◄ Two young British women aboard a ship carrying emigrants to Australia in the 1940s.

▲ A 1950s-style American car at a wedding in the "Rocks" area of Sydney shows the influence of the United States on Australia.

New Zealand, and the United States. SEATO linked the ANZUS countries, Britain, France, Thailand, Pakistan, Cambodia, South Vietnam, and Laos, in an anticommunist alliance.

Between 1950 and the 1970s, Australia sent troops to help U.S. forces in wars in Korea and Vietnam. The Vietnam War became unpopular with many Australians, who wanted to know why their young men needed to be sent to fight in a country with which they had no quarrel. Australia's warm relationship with the United States cooled when Australian troops were brought home from the Vietnam War in 1972. U.S forces remained in Vietnam until 1975.

The support of Australia's government for U.S.-led invasions of Afghanistan, in 2001, and Iraq, in 2003, cemented friendly relations with the United States once more. Possibly as a result of this support, Australia made a free-trade agreement with the United States in 2005.

UN INVOLVEMENT

Australia is strongly involved in United Nations (UN) activities, including human rights work, economic development, weapons control, the fight against the trade in illegal drugs, and peacekeeping. In September 1999, Australia led an international UN peacekeeping force in East Timor. Indonesia's forces occupied East Timor in 1975, and the East Timorese people accused them of many human rights abuses. In 1999, East Timor voted to become independent, but in an act of revenge Indonesian militias began

 Did You Know?

About 29,000 Australians died in action during World War II.

attacking the East Timorese people. Australia led the UN force that restored order and helped the country to become independent in May 2002.

REGIONAL ORGANIZATIONS

Australia has recently played a peacekeeping role in Papua New Guinea and the Solomon Islands. These countries are fellow members of the Pacific Islands Forum, an organization that connects countries in the Pacific region. Members of the forum cooperate in efforts to maintain security, improve living standards, and ensure sustainable development.

Australia works to develop close links with many of its Asian neighbors, and it is part of the Association of Southeast Asian Nations Regional Forum. Australia gives over U.S. $1 billion a year in aid to poorer countries, much of which is distributed in Asia. Papua New Guinea, Thailand, and Indonesia all received substantial aid packages from the country in the 1990s, and Australia provided immediate help to the Asian countries affected by the huge tsunami of December 2004. Australia's links in the Asian Pacific also help in its trading relations with countries such as Japan and China, among others.

THE COMMONWEALTH

In addition to regional links, Australia is an active member of the Commonwealth, a group of countries that were once governed by Britain. The Commonwealth connects wealthy countries, such as Australia and Britain, with poorer countries to try to help cultural understanding and economic development. It also organizes the Commonwealth Games, which Australia has hosted four times, most recently in 2006 in Melbourne, Victoria.

The Commonwealth is less important for trade than it once was, but Australia still retains trade links with many Commonwealth countries.

 Did You Know?

Australia was one of the countries that helped draft the charter of the United Nations, which was signed in 1945.

◀ Members of a peacekeeping force— including an Australian soldier in the foreground—carry out a security patrol of Dili's Airport in East Timor at the beginning of UN Operation Stabilize in 1999.

Focus on: Terrorism and the Muslim world

During the late 1990s and into the twenty-first century, Australia became increasingly unpopular in the Muslim world. One reason for this was that it supported the U.S.-led invasions of Afghanistan and Iraq, both Muslim countries.

Another reason was that it had given support to East Timor, whose mainly Catholic population had demanded independence from mainly Muslim Indonesian control. In October 2002, a terrorist bombing on the island of Bali in Indonesia killed 202 people. Bali is a favorite vacation spot for Australians, and 89 Australians were killed in the attack. Islamic terrorists claimed responsibility for the Bali bombing. In 2005, a second bombing in Bali killed 23 people, including four Australians.

Australia's generous aid to victims of the 2004 tsunami resulted in an increase in its popularity in Asian Muslim countries. At the same time, Australia toughened up its immigration policies in the hope of keeping Islamic extremists out of the country.

◀ This memorial to the victims of the Bali bombing stands at Coogee Beach, in Sydney.

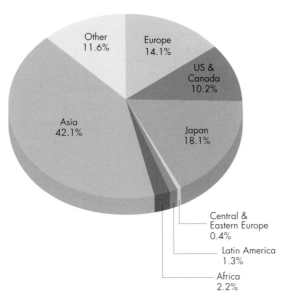

▲ Destination of exports by major trading region

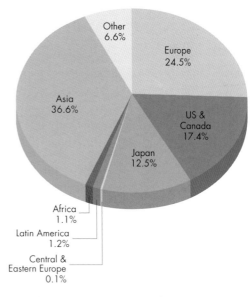

▲ Origin of imports by major trading region

Transportation and Communications

Australia's huge size and the inhospitable climate of its interior have always made it uncomfortable and sometimes dangerous to travel long distances within the country. The first European settlers to arrive in Australia took many years to break out of Sydney and through the barrier of the Blue Mountains. All of Australia's first settlements were on good harbors, because it was far easier to move from place to place by sea than overland.

Even today, the areas between some of the country's settlements are large and inhospitable. People planning to drive in the interior of some areas of Western Australia, for example, are warned to carry extra water and food with them, because if their car breaks down, they may have a long wait before help arrives. Australian transportation routes tend to link together the main settlements. Exceptions include roads or railways that have been built to reach industrial sites, such as mines.

Transport & Communications Data

- Total roads: 504,330 miles/811,603 km
- Total paved roads: 195,175 miles/ 314,090 km
- Total unpaved roads: 309,155 miles/ 497,513 km
- Total railways: 33,828 miles/54,439 km
- Airports: 448
- Cars per 1,000 people: 635
- Cellular phones per 1,000 people: 719.5
- Personal computers per 1,000 people: 565.1
- Internet users per 1,000 people: 566.7

Source: World Bank and CIA World Factbook

WATER TRANSPORTATION

Water transportation remains an important link between Australia's coastal cities. Ships carry large amounts of minerals along the coasts, and

◀ Giant cranes load and unload containers from ships at Melbourne's international port.

▶ A double-decker train pulls into Summer Hill Suburban Station, ready to carry commuters to work in Sydney.

most of Australia's overseas exports are sent by sea. In the country's east, Gladstone, Hay Point, Melbourne, Newcastle, and Sydney are among the busiest ports. The use of Sydney Harbor as a port, however, has been under debate partly because of fears that it could be a terrorist target. In Australia's west, the busiest ports include Dampier, Fremantle, Port Hedland, and Port Walcott.

RAIL TRANSPORTATION

Main rail lines connect many of Australia's major cities and towns, particularly in the country's east. Trains mostly carry freight, but many also carry passengers. Sydney and Melbourne have extensive networks of local train lines, which provide a fast and inexpensive way to move around the city.

All of Australia's main railway lines are government owned. The country also has a small number of privately owned railways. These usually belong to mining companies and are used to transport minerals from the mines to a main railway line.

 Did You Know?

The Trans-Australian Railway has the longest stretch of straight track in the world.

Focus on: The Trans-Australian Railway

The Trans-Australian Railway is the longest rail line in Australia. It stretches 1,108 miles (1,783 km) from Port Pirie, in South Australia, to Kalgoorlie, in Western Australia. Work began at each end of the line in 1913, and the two sections finally met on October 17, 1917. Today, the journey takes 37 hours and passes through some of Australia's most distinctive landscapes.

Heading east from Kalgoorlie, the train crosses a plateau that is mostly forested with eucalyptus trees. Next, it reaches a treeless area where only low bushes grow. Part of this is the Nullarbor Plain, through which the line runs straight for 309 miles (497 km). Finally, the train heads across the red soil and low hills of South Australia toward Port Pirie.

AIR TRAVEL

Australia has an extensive network of airports. The main cities each have international airports, and there are also smaller terminals for flights within Australia. In Outback areas, a large sheep station may have its own small aircraft and a landing strip for small planes. Some farmers even use helicopters in crop herding.

ROAD TRANSPORT

Most Australian families own at least one car, which is their main way of getting around. The cities have excellent road networks, although, with so much car use, they can become very crowded at busy times of the day, especially when people are traveling to and from work. Long traffic jams are common, and it can be as quick to walk as to drive short distances through city centers.

Major towns and cities are connected by a good series of mainly two-lane roads. Minor roads outside developed areas are often unpaved, as are many of the roads in the Outback. Instead, people drive along leveled dirt tracks.

Cycling any distance in the heat of the Outback is not very practical. But many Australian cities are eager to increase cycle use because cycling is healthy and does not cause pollution or congestion. Few city streets, however, are designed for cycling, and Australian drivers are not particularly aware of the safety of cyclists. The introduction of cycle routes will encourage more people to get on their bikes, and an increasing number of routes are being completed each year.

MODERN COMMUNICATIONS

Almost one out of three Australians buys a newspaper every day, compared with, for example, one out of five Americans. As a result, Australians are generally well informed. They also receive regular news updates on TV. Australia had one telephone line for every two people in 2001. More than half of Australians own a personal computer and use the Internet.

▼ An airplane stands in front of the domestic departure terminal at Sydney Airport. Low-cost airlines have made traveling around Australia cheaper and faster than ever before.

These numbers have grown rapidly and continue to do so. Modern communications technologies such as telephones, cellular phones, and e-mail have revolutionized life for many Australians, especially those in the Outback or other remote areas. Previously, buying nonlocal goods might have involved a long journey. Today, it is possible to browse a Web site or catalog, pick up the phone or go online, and order whatever you want. Medical advice and education are also available via the Internet and e-mail, and people in isolated communities can make contact with others who have similar interests, even if they live thousands of miles apart.

? Did You Know?

In 2005, Australia had 142 airports with unpaved runways.

▲ An opal miner uses a solar powered phone in a Queensland Outback town. Modern telecommunications such as this are extremely important in the more remote areas of Australia.

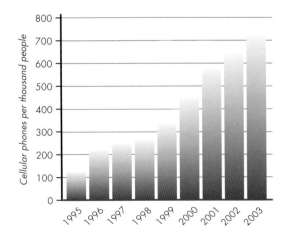

▲ Cellular phone use, 1995–2003

CHAPTER 10

Education and Health

Each state or territory in Australia runs its own education system, which is paid for with federal funds. The country's education system, therefore, varies slightly in different states and territories. For example, amounts of time students spend in primary or secondary school vary. Everywhere, education is divided between primary, secondary, and post-secondary levels. All schools across Australia must follow national curriculum guidelines.

STANDARDS OF LITERACY

Australia generally has a high standard of education and high literacy rates. However, one out of five adults in the country lacks some reading and writing skills and, as a result, finds it difficult to participate in everyday life. Indigenous Australians have a poor record of educational achievement and, in the past, have found it difficult to do well in school. Many Indigenous Australians saw school as an unwelcoming place in which the language, clothing, and behavior were completely different from what they were used to. Even today, over 10 percent of Indigenous Australian children do not go to school, and those who do generally have lower than average reading skills by their third year. In the Northern Territory, only about 25 percent of Indigenous Australian children reached the target standard, versus 65 percent of other students.

STATE AND PRIVATE SCHOOLS

In state-owned and run schools, education is said to be free. Many state-run schools in Australia, however, charge parents a small amount. The country's private schools, many of which are owned and run by the Roman Catholic Church,

Did You Know?

The King's School in Sydney is the oldest independent school in Australia. It was founded in 1831.

▼ This picture shows a typical classroom in an Australian primary school.

charge significantly higher fees for attendance. The country's private schools have become increasingly popular, because they are thought by some to offer a better education. Students at both state and private schools usually have to wear uniforms, although this is not always the case. Private schools tend to have stricter dress codes.

Many children in Australia begin school at about 3 years old, when they go to kindergarten or "preprimary." All children must start primary school by 6 years old. They stay in primary school for between 6 and 8 years and then progress to secondary school—which is generally called high school—for 5 or 6 years. The minimum age at which they can leave school varies between 15 and 16.

After high school, students can go on to post-secondary education. One option is a one- or two-year vocational training course at an institute of technical education, where they can study a trade such as car mechanics or agricultural science. Other students choose a three- or four-year degree course at a university, studying anything from English literature to chemistry. Graduates of postsecondary education find it easier to obtain work than those who leave school at age 16.

LONG-DISTANCE LEARNING

Many Australian children living in Outback areas are too far from schools to be able to attend. Instead, they take correspondence courses. In the past, these courses were taken by mail. Today, they usually use the Internet. Every state and territory has a correspondence school for children in isolated locations. Three states and the Northern Territory also have "schools of the air," through which children can contact their teachers directly by radio, fax, or computer.

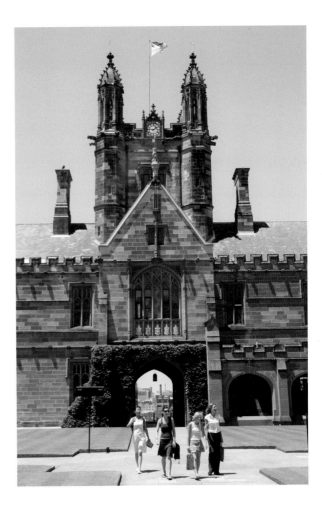

▲ Students stroll outside a building of a university in Sydney.

Education and Health Data

- Life expectancy at birth, male: 76.9
- Life expectancy at birth, female: 82.7
- Infant mortality rate per 1,000: 6
- Under-five mortality rate per 1,000: 6
- Physicians per 1,000 people: 2.5
- Health expenditure as % of GDP: 9.5%
- Education expenditure as % of GDP: 4.9%
- Primary school net enrollment: 96%
- Student-teacher ratio, primary: n/a
- Adult literacy as % age 15+: 99%

Source: United Nations Agencies and World Bank

◀ Today, doctors can use the Internet to give advice to patients in isolated areas of Australia.

HEALTH CARE

Health care is provided by each of Australia's states and territories, using money that comes mainly from the federal government. National health-care policies are decided at the federal level. All residents of Australia are entitled to free health care at public hospitals, under a program called Medicare. Medicare also pays for 85 percent of the cost of going to see a general practitioner. Medicare is paid for mainly by a 1.5 percent tax on people's incomes.

Australians can also choose private medical care, either by paying for their treatment directly or by buying private health insurance. Private health insurance involves paying a monthly fee to an insurance company that, in return, will pay for future medical costs. As in almost every country, wealthier people in Australia tend to get higher quality medical treatment. They also tend to receive the care they need more quickly than the poor.

NATIONAL AND LOCAL FUNCTIONS

Australia's federal government provides money for public hospitals, residential care facilities, and home and community care. It also pays for most of the country's health research and supports the training of health professionals. State and territory governments provide the actual health services, including most hospitals. The states and territories also run a range of community and public health services, including health services in schools; dental clinics; care for mothers and children, such as pre- and postnatal classes; and disease control programs. Local government is mostly involved in environmental health issues, such as garbage disposal, clean water, and some health inspections.

STRAINS ON THE SYSTEM

Almost 10 percent of Australia's GDP is spent on health care. This money is being stretched further each year, mainly as a result of demands by Australia's ageing population. People are living longer, and, as people get older, they need more health-care services. At the same time, Australians generally are having fewer children than they did 30 years ago. Because of this, there will be fewer taxpayers to contribute to Medicare in the future. Dealing with this issue is likely to present Australia's government with a significant challenge in the future.

 Did You Know?

Before the Flying Doctors, medical help in the Outback was usually provided by "Boundary Riders"—who often traveled by camel.

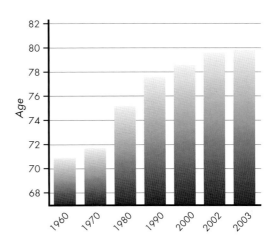

▲ Life expectancy at birth, 1960–2003

Focus on: The Flying Doctors

The Flying Doctors—or, to use the group's full name, the Royal Flying Doctor Service—provides health care services to people in remote communities. Founded in 1928 by the Reverend John Flynn, the Flying Doctors treat roughly 183,000 people a year. They have 17 bases, 38 aircraft, and fly over 2,759,900 sq miles (7,150,000 sq km) of territory. In addition to flying into remote areas, the Flying Doctors provide medical advice by radio and telephone.

Running the Flying Doctors costs about AUS$43 million each year and is paid for mainly by grants from the federal, state, and territory governments. Donations from businesses and the general public also help to keep the service going.

◀ A member of the Flying Doctors transfers a patient from a light aircraft to a waiting ambulance.

CHAPTER 11

Culture and Religion

Australia's original culture is that of the Indigenous Australians, but they are now largely marginalized from society. Very little traditional Indigenous Australian culture and religion spilled into the lives of the country's early settlers or immigrant Australians.

Since the 1960s, however, Indigenous Australian art has become increasingly sought after in Australia and around the world. The close relationship to the land that is a key part of Indigenous Australian beliefs inspires some of Australia's environmental campaigners. It has also influenced filmmakers, such as Nicolas Roeg (*Walkabout*) and Phillip Noyce (*Rabbit-Proof Fence*). Indigenous Australian actors such as Ernie Dingo and musicians such as Yothu Yindi have also been successful.

RELIGION

Australia's constitution forbids a state religion and guarantees people freedom of worship. Most Australians are Christian—typically either Anglican or Roman Catholic—but few people in the country attend church regularly. The Uniting Church, which was formed by Methodists, Congregationalists, and Presbyterians in 1977, is Australia's third-largest Christian church. There are also small Jewish

▼ Les Saxby, an Indigenous Australian musician, plays a traditional instrument known as a didgeridoo. He is playing on the shore of Botany Bay, at the exact spot where Captain Cook's expedition first landed in Australia in 1788. Each year, the Meeting of Two Cultures ceremony takes place at this location. It is attended by local community groups.

and Muslim communities in Australia's cities. More than 16.6 percent of Australians are atheist or claim no religion at all.

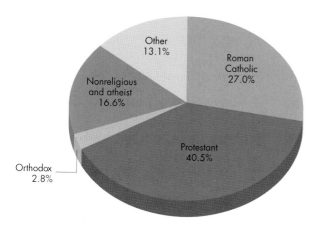

▲ Australia's major religions

LITERATURE

Australia is home to some of the great writers of the twentieth and twenty-first centuries. The novelist Patrick White, for example, won the Nobel Prize for Literature in 1973. Another author, Thomas Keneally, wrote the novel *Schindler's List*, on which Steven Spielberg's famous film was based. Peter Carey has won many international awards. His book *Illywacker* tells the story of Australia in the early days of the twentieth century, not long after it became a united country. Today, many people think Tim Winton—whose novels, including *The Turning* and *Cloudstreet*, have won many awards—is one of the most talented novelists around.

ART

Art, and especially painting, is one area in which Indigenous Australian culture has spread beyond the Aboriginal community. Indigenous Australian paintings are popular both within Australia and internationally, with artists such as Albert Namatjira and Emily Kngwarreye having become well known around the world. Australia's best-known non-Aboriginal artists are probably Sidney Nolan, Fred Williams, and Russell Drysdale. Drysdale is famous for his pictures of the Outback.

► Author Thomas Keneally works in the study of his home on the northern beaches of Sydney in 2001.

FILM

At the start of the twentieth century, Australia was one of the first countries in the world to have a film industry. The industry died out during the 1920s and 1930s but has come back to life and now produces about 20 feature films a year. Notable Australian directors include Peter Weir and Bruce Beresford. Australia is probably better known, however, as home to actors such as Russell Crowe, Nicole Kidman, and Guy Pearce.

MUSIC AND THEATER

Australia has national opera and ballet companies, and some of its big cities have their own orchestras and dance companies. State capitals also have their own theater companies, and Australia's international theater festivals are world famous. Australia's most famous popular music performer is probably the singer Kylie Minogue. Australia's successful international acts also include the bands INXS and AC/DC.

 Did You Know?

Some people claim that an Australian film made in 1906 was the world's first feature film. Entitled *The Story of the Kelly Gang*, it was a six-minute fictional account of Australian folk-hero Ned Kelly.

SPORTS

Sport is the glue that binds Australians, especially men, together. Whether playing as amateurs or watching professional sports, Australians take sports very seriously. For a country with a relatively small population, Australia is phenomenally successful at an incredible range of sports.

The country's most popular game is probably Australian Rules football, a tough game based

▼ Singer Kylie Minogue performs on stage in 2004.

around kicking, punching, or tapping an oval ball. Each team has 18 players, and they aim to score points by getting goals, or "behinds." The country has a professional Australian Rules football league made up of teams coming from throughout the country. At first difficult for non-Australians to understand, this fast-moving game is very exciting to watch.

The list of sports in which Australia's athletes and teams are among the world's best is long. It includes swimming, cricket, rugby, netball, cycling, hockey, surfing, car racing, motorcycle racing, cycling, and tennis. The Socceroos, Australia's national soccer team, reached the second round of the 2006 World Cup. Australia, with very limited snow sports facilities, has even managed to produce some excellent skiers and snowboarders.

 Did You Know?

Almost seven million people went to see Australian Rules football matches in 2005.

Focus on: The Sydney Olympics

In 2000, Sydney hosted the Olympic Games. They were the most successful—or, at least, the most watched—sports event in history. About 3.7 billion people watched them from 220 different countries and territories. Part of the reason for the success of the Games was the city of Sydney and its people. Many Sydneysiders volunteered to help make sure the huge numbers of athletes and visitors to the city had a good time. Sports-crazy Australians bought almost every available ticket: 92 percent were sold, a huge improvement on the previous record of 82 percent set during the Games in Atlanta in 1996. Even events that are usually hard sells, such as early rounds of the swimming competitions, packed the arenas. Possibly as a result, the athletes gave some exciting performances. The International Olympic Committee chairman said the Sydney Olympics were,"the best Games ever." Many people agreed with him.

◀ A volleyball player "digs" the ball at the 2000 Olympics in Sydney.

CHAPTER 12

Leisure and Tourism

Most Australians are fortunate to live in a warm, mainly dry climate. It is rarely very cold, and the coastal areas are rarely too hot. Australia is an easy place to spend a lot of time outdoors and, as a result, its people have a real love of what is often called "the outdoor life." In general, Australians love to socialize outdoors, and sport is an important part of this. Playing sports, cooking and eating outdoors, camping, and spending time at the beach or in the countryside are all popular activities with many Australians. Walking in the country's wild scrub or forest lands—the bush—is increasingly popular, especially in spectacular locations such as the Blue Mountains.

THE BEACH

The beach is an important part of life for many Australians. With so many cities on or near the country's beaches, most Australians live within a relatively short distance to the seaside. They head for the beaches on Sundays for family barbecues. Many beaches have coin-operated public grills, in which a small amount of money buys some cooking time. Nearby are tables and chairs, some with shelter in case of wind or rain, at which people can sit and eat what they have cooked. To prepare for another popular

▼ A crowd watches a free Sunday concert outdoors in Melbourne in 2005.

Australian pastime—surfing—many children go to "Little Nippers" surf lifesaving classes that are held at certain beaches. Surfing is a lifetime obsession for many Australians.

 Did You Know?

Swimming in the sea on Sundays was illegal in Australia until the early twentieth century because it was considered immodest.

SURFING

Australia is home to some of the world's best surf breaks, or recognized spots where people go surfing. Bell's Beach, in Victoria; the giant surf of Margaret River, in Western Australia; and the waves at Kirra, on the country's west coast attract surfers from around the world. Almost every coastal settlement on Australia's west, south, or east coasts has a surf break. It is no wonder that Australia has produced some of the world's best surfers, including several world champions.

▼ A surfer rides a wave at Avalon Beach, which is located in New South Wales.

EATING OUT

"Barbies" are outdoor get-togethers based around cooking food on a barbecue. Guests often bring some food along, with everyone adding a little something to make a giant feast. To anyone not used to Australian barbies, the large amounts of meat that get cooked and eaten—including burgers, sausages, chops, and steaks—can be amazing.

Eating at restaurants is also popular among Australians, especially in the cities. Even in the cities, people often take the opportunity to eat outside if they can. Australia is famous for its delicious "fusion" cooking, which combines Western and Asian flavors.

MUSEUMS AND GALLERIES

Australia's big cities—Melbourne, Sydney, and Canberra, in particular—have excellent museums and art galleries. Their museums and galleries mount permanent displays of their own, and they also often host visiting exhibitions from abroad. Many major traveling exhibitions of art make a stop in Australia.

TOURISM

Australia is popular among international travelers. Most of its visitors come from New Zealand (21 percent), Japan (15 percent), Britain (14 percent), the United States (9 percent), and China (6 percent). In addition, 23 percent of its visitors come from other countries in Asia, mainly those in Southeast Asia, and 12 percent come from mainland Europe. Australians also like to travel within their own country, and many tourists are from elsewhere in Australia.

Foreign travelers visit Australia for a variety of reasons, including vacations, visits to relatives, and business or work in Australia. The top activities for tourists in the country include shopping; going to the beach (including going swimming, surfing, and diving); and visiting markets, pubs, clubs and discos. Tourists also visit Australia's national parks, state parks, wildlife parks, zoos, aquariums, and botanical gardens. In addition, some may take a charter, cruise, or ferry boat; visit heritage sites or monuments; or take guided tours or excursions.

Sydney is by far the most popular city for tourists to visit, with over half of the visitors to Australia staying there for an average of 15 nights. The city's biggest attractions are the Opera House, the Sydney Harbor Bridge, and the Darling Harbor complex of restaurants and shops. Australia's most popular noncity areas are the tropical and semitropical parts of its east coast, located in northern New South Wales and Queensland. Offshore in this region is the Great Barrier Reef, which attracts visiting divers and snorkelers from around the world.

Focus on: Ecotourism

Ecotourists come to experience Australia's natural environment, whether by taking a whale-watching trip, walking in its national parks, or doing some other activity. The number of ecotourists has grown each year since 2000. By 2003, over 60 percent of Australia's international visitors were taking part in ecotourism activities.

◀ Tourists pose for a photo with the Sydney Harbor Bridge and the Opera House in the background.

OTHER MAJOR ATTRACTIONS

Many people visit Australia without going to see particular attractions. The country is, however, home to some incredible tourist sites that draw visitors from around the world.

Uluru, or Ayers Rock, a giant rock formation in the desert at the center of Australia, has been used for years on posters for Australia's tourist industry. Almost every morning and evening, this site is busy with visitors. Other natural tourist attractions include the Blue Mountains, located west of Sydney. The spectacular rock escarpments and beautiful walking trails in these mountains are popular with visitors. In Victoria, the Great Ocean Road winds alongside the sea on its way past the spectacular Twelve Apostles, a dramatic group of rock pillars that stands in the ocean.

▶ These tourists are taking a sightseeing tour of the Sydney Harbor Bridge. They are required to put on gray suits that blend in with the bridge so that views of the bridge from elsewhere are not spoiled.

 Did You Know?

More than one million people have climbed the Sydney Harbor Bridge.

Tourism in Australia

- Tourist arrivals, millions: 5.215
- Earnings from tourism in U.S.$: 14,528,000,000
- Tourism as % foreign earnings: 15.9
- Tourist departures, millions: 3.388
- Expenditure on tourism in U.S.$: 10,136,000,512

Source: World Bank

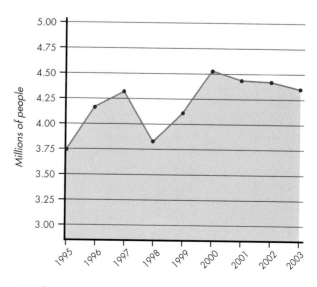

▲ Changes in international tourism, 1995–2003

CHAPTER 13

Environment and Conservation

Australia is home to a unique environment. Separated from other landmasses about 200 million years ago, its plants and animals developed completely differently from those anywhere else in the world. The country has thousands of species that exist in Australia and nowhere else. Australia's best known animals include kangaroos, koalas, echidnas, platypuses, cockatoos, and emus. The country's distinctive plants and trees include eucalyptus trees and acacias.

A FRAGILE ECOSYSTEM

Australia's natural environment, particularly in areas with little rainfall, is fragile. It's balance has developed over vast stretches of time. Sudden changes of any kind put such a strain on the environment that it quickly reaches a breaking point. For example, wells for new houses can quickly exhaust underground water supplies that have nourished plants for thousands of years. Increases in population, including increases in the numbers of tourists, are also putting the environment under increased strain. For example, areas such as the Blue Mountains and the Great Barrier Reef are being damaged by the presence of tens of thousands of tourists each year.

LOSS OF HABITAT

Of course, humans have been living in, and changing, the environment of Australia for a long time. But all the major environmental changes have happened since the European settlers arrived about 200 years ago. In the last 200 years, 40 percent of Australia's forests have been cleared, and 70 percent of its native vegetation has been lost.

Loss of these habitats has had a serious effect on the animals that adapted to them over millions of years. Another problem for native animals and plants is the introduction of new species from outside Australia. One example of this is the rabbit, which ruined crops and natural vegetation—and deprived native species of

◀ Koalas live only in Australia. They feed on eucalyptus leaves, and they can only survive where these trees grow.

food—before its numbers were brought under control. The combination of losing habitats with competition or hunting by new species has had a terrible effect on Australia's native species. Animals such as the tree kangaroo, the numbat, the greater bilby, and the quoll are either extinct or on the verge of extinction.

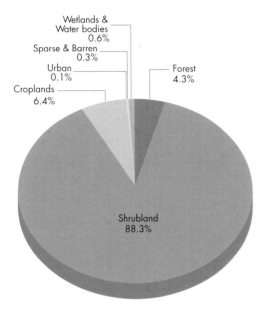

Wetlands & Water bodies 0.6%
Sparse & Barren 0.3%
Urban 0.1%
Croplands 6.4%
Forest 4.3%
Shrubland 88.3%

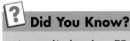
▲ Habitat type as a percentage of total area

Did You Know?

Australia has lost 75 percent of its rain forests in the last 200 years.

Focus on: Tasmania's Forests

Tasmania has some of the oldest and tallest hardwood forests in Australia. These are a valuable resource, and logging companies have been removing the old-growth trees at a rate of about 49,420 acres (20,000 hectares) every year. Environmentalists are fighting a long, bitter campaign to save Tasmania's forests. They point out that, although the logging is profitable, it costs Tasmania in other ways. For example, endangered species such as the Tasmanian wedge-tailed eagle; the giant freshwater crayfish, which is the world's largest type of crayfish; and the "tiger cat," or spotted-tail quoll, are losing their habitats. Another problem is that the cut-down forests are not being replaced. Instead, the logging companies plant rows of different types of trees, which they will cut down in 15 to 20 years. The logging companies also use poison to clear the plantations of animals that eat young saplings, and the poison kills anything coming into contact with it.

▼ A rainstorm waters an area of pastureland in the state of Victoria.

SUSTAINABILITY

Sustainability means use of natural resources in a way that will make it possible for other people to enjoy them in the future. Some people believe Australians live unsustainable lifestyles in many ways. Sydney, for example, currently uses water at a rate of 108 percent of its water resources. For every 10.6 quarts (10 liters) of water available from rainfall, rivers, and other sources, 11.4 quarts (10.8 liters) get used. Concern exists that if use continues at this rate, Sydney's water reserves will be used up. Another example is that Australians are using the continent's supplies of groundwater at a far faster rate than they are being replaced. Showers, swimming pools, flush toilets, and other high-water-use facilities come at a cost to the environment. Few people, however, are willing to give them up, in spite of the fact some commentators think that the water will one day run out if it continues to be used at the same rate as today. There is, however, no projected date by when this might happen.

WASTE

Australians are among the most wasteful people on Earth in terms of the amount of actual waste they create per person. The only country more wasteful than Australia is the United States. More than 19.8 million tons (18 million metric tons) of household waste are sent to Australia's landfill sites each year. According to one source, this is enough waste to cover the entire state of Victoria in a layer almost 4 inches (100 mm) deep. At some point, Victoria's landfill will become visible over the city's horizon.

NO TO KYOTO

In 1997, many of the world's nations signed the Kyoto Protocol on Climate Change. This document aimed to reduce the amount of greenhouse gases released into the environment, with each country setting a target for how

▼ Australia's high levels of water use—for example, in private swimming pools—may not be sustainable in the future.

much their greenhouse emissions would change. Most wealthy countries aimed to reduce their emissions, but Australia insisted on being allowed to increase its emissions by 8 percent and did not sign the protocol.

POSITIVE NEWS

In spite of all this, Australia was ranked thirteenth in the world in the 2005 Environmental Sustainability Index. In 1999, the Environment Protection and Biodiversity Conservation Act, which aims to protect threatened species, became law. National and state parks offer some protection of Australia's unique ecosystems; 64 wetlands are registered under the Ramsar Convention; and 16 world heritage sites have been established.

On an individual level, many Australians are trying to live in more sustainable ways, especially in less built-up areas. Composting toilets are increasingly popular, and solar panels or windmills are being used to provide power. In the cities, many people are trying to use cars less. State governments are insisting that new buildings be located near public transportation to reduce car use and be built to use less energy.

Organizations such as the Australian Conservation Foundation, the Wilderness Society, and the Australian Trust for Conservation Volunteers work on projects aimed at protecting Australia's environment. Visitors to Australia can now participate in the Willing Workers On Organic Farms program; this is called going "WWOOFing."

Environmental and Conservation Data

- 📂 Forested area as % total land area: 4.3
- 📂 Protected area as % total land area: 7.5
- 📂 Number of protected areas: 4,487

SPECIES DIVERSITY

Category	Known species	Threatened species
Mammals	252	63
Breeding birds	497	37
Reptiles	876	38
Amphibians	228	35
Fish	1,489	44
Plants	15,638	38

Source: World Resources Institute

▶ The Bungle Bungles are a maze of narrow gorges and secluded gullies that are accessible to ecotourists by walking trails. They are rich in Aboriginal culture and history.

CHAPTER 14

Future Challenges

What does the future hold for Australia? On the positive side, the country has a number of advantages. Because it produces almost all its own food, it does not have to rely on imports to feed its people. It has a number of valuable natural resources, leading the world in some of them. If, as fossil fuels run out, the world becomes more dependent on nuclear power, Australia's extensive uranium deposits will become increasingly valuable.

MAINTAINING TOLERANCE

Australia has largely been able to accept immigrants without the problems of ghettoization and resentment that have resulted from large scale immigration in other countries. Australia is generally a tolerant and friendly place, though at times there have been conflicts between its Australian-born and its immigrant communities. In 2005, for example, there were clashes on Sydney's southern beaches between white Australians and Lebanese-Australians.

Australia does, however, face a number of major challenges in the future. Among these are its economy, the situation of the Indigenous Australian people, its environment, and the threat of terrorism.

▼ In 2005, Olympic gold medalist Cathy Freeman (left) took part in the "Long Walk," a march to support the rights of Indigenous Australian people.

THE ECONOMY

Australia is a wealthy country with a strong economy. Many of its exports, however, are raw materials such as iron, coal, or food animals. These exports are vulnerable to competition from elsewhere in the world, and their value is affected by prices on world markets. Meanwhile, many of its imports are high-value manufactured goods, which are more expensive in relative terms. Australia's government is trying to encourage growth in the production and export of manufactured goods, rather than raw materials, to increase the country's income.

INDIGENOUS AUSTRALIANS

Indigenous Australians have the lowest standard of living of any group in Australian society. Australia likes to see itself as a fair society, but the situation of its original inhabitants argues that this is not always the case. Many people are working to improve the lives of Indigenous Australians.

THE ENVIRONMENT

Some practices in Australia are not sustainable. In such a fragile environment this could be disastrous, first for the plants and animals of the continent and, later, for its people. One challenge is to persuade people to give up some of the creature comforts that make life in a sometimes harsh environment more pleasant.

TERRORISM

Some of Australia's international actions—such as its support of the invasions of Afghanistan and Iraq and its role in East Timor—have made it a target for terrorist attacks by Islamic extremists. The attacks in Bali in 2002 and 2005, for example, were aimed largely at Western tourists, many of whom were Australians. Australia will need to adopt international policies and security measures to prevent further terrorist attacks.

▼ With Sydney's business district and botanical gardens behind them, joggers run by the water.

Time Line

200 million years ago The Australian continent breaks away, as Earth's continents slowly move apart. From this time on, Australia is an isolated landmass.

40,000–60,000 years ago The first humans arrive in Australia from Asia.

1606 Dutch navigator Willem Jansz makes the first confirmed sighting of Australia.

1642–1643 Dutch navigator Abel Tasman sails around Australia without sighting the mainland. He discovers Tasmania, which he names Van Diemen's Land.

1688 Former buccaneer William Dampier lands on Australia's northwest coast, near King Sound in what is now Western Australia. He records what he sees in a journal.

1770 British Navy captain James Cook sights and explores the fertile east coast of Australia. Cook claims the land for Britain and names it New South Wales.

1787 Captain Arthur Phillip—with 570 male convicts, 160 female convicts, about 200 British soldiers, about 30 wives of soldiers, and a few children—sets sail for New South Wales to establish a prison colony. The group travels in 11 ships, called the First Fleet.

1788 The first ship reaches Botany Bay, on Australia's east coast, on January 18, 1788. Phillip's ship arrives on January 19, and the rest arrive on January 20. The colony's first settlement is near a large harbor about 7 miles (11 km) north of Botany Bay, the current site of the city of Sydney.

1790s The British colonial government gives military officers and freed convicts permission to settle lands in Australia.

1803–1863 Various additional settlements and territories are established, including Melbourne in the 1830s.

1851 Gold is discovered, first, in New South Wales and, later, in Victoria.

1860 Robert Burke and William Wills lead an expedition across Australia's interior. Both men die on the return journey from the north coast.

1868 Britain ends it practice of "transportation," or sending convicts to Australia. By this time, more than 160,000 people had been sent to Australia.

1899–1902 Australian armed forces are involved in fighting, on behalf of the British in the Boer War in South Africa.

1901 The Commonwealth of Australia is formed, making Australia a united country for the first time.

1914–1918 Thousands of Australian men travel to Europe to fight in World War I.

1939–1945 Australia fights both in Europe and the Pacific region during World War II. More than 29,000 Australian service people are killed.

1950–1953 Australian troops support the United States in the Korean War.

1964 Conscription is introduced in Australia. Young Australian men are sent to fight on the side of the United States in the Vietnam War.

1967 Prime Minister Harold Holt disappears while swimming in the sea near Melbourne. Rumors abound that Holt was abducted by a Chinese submarine, but it was later revealed that he drowned.

1972 Australia's relations with the United States are strained when it brings its troops home from Vietnam.

1975 The British Queen's unelected representative in Australia, Governor General Sir John Kerr, removes the democratically elected prime minister, Gough Whitlam, sparking a crisis.

1990s Prime Minister Paul Keating recommends that Australia cut its ties with Britain and become a republic.

1999 In a referendum on whether they want their country to remain a constitutional monarchy or to become a republic, the people of Australia decide to keep the monarchy. Australia leads an international force to help the territory of East Timor become independent of Indonesia.

2001 Australia supports the invasion of Afghanistan.

2002 A bombing by Islamic terrorists on the Indonesian island of Bali claims the lives of 89 Australians.

2003 Australia supports the U.S.-led invasion of Iraq.

2005 Another terrorist bombing in Bali kills 4 Australians.

Glossary

animal husbandry the practice of farming animals

ANZUS a defense agreement signed by Australia, New Zealand, and the United States in 1951, in which the countries pledged that an attack on one country would represent an assault on all three

arable capable of being used for growing crops

arid excessively dry; technically, receiving less than 10 inches (25 centimeters) of rain per year

capital wealth in the form of property or money, especially money available for investment

Cold War the period of hostility between the United States and the Soviet Union between the end of World War II and 1991, during which the two countries built up their militaries and worked to support their political systems in other countries and conflicts around the world

colonial having to do with or belonging to a colony

colony a settlement that is under the political control of another country, often founded by and populated largely by people from that country

Commonwealth Australia's name for its federal union of states; also the group of countries to which Australia belongs that have the British monarch as head of state

communism an economic system in which the means of production, distribution, and exchange are controlled by the state

communist a follower of communism

conscription the practice of forcing people to join an armed force for a set period of time

constitutional monarchy a system of government in which the head of state is a king or queen, but power is held by an elected body

crust Earth's hard outer layer

Diggers Australian soldiers, many of whom took part in World War I and who are greatly admired in their country; so called either because many of them had been gold miners or because of their trench-digging activities during the war

ecosystem a group of plants and animals that depend on one another and the land on which they live to survive

eucalyptus a type of tall evergreen tree that grows mainly in Australia

federation a government of a large area that has been formed by an alliance between smaller states or territories and in which the member states or territories may have some degree of independence in their internal affairs

free trade trade between countries or territories without any taxes on the goods that go from one to another

geologists scientists who study the history of Earth, especially through its rocks

ghettoization the creation of usually poor communities of people who are isolated from the rest of society

Gross Domestic Product (GDP) the total value of goods and services produced within a country

Gross National Income (GNI) the total value of a country's income from goods and services produced by its residents both within the country and elsewhere in the world

groundwater water in natural underground reservoirs that supplies wells and springs

irrigation the use of water supplied by artificial routes to help crops grow

kinship group a group of people who recognize that they are all related to one another

militia a military group made up of members of the general population to assist the army in an emergency or other group of citizens organized for military service

ocher an earthy yellow-orange color

opal a semiprecious stone found in large quantities in Australia

plateau a high, flat area of land

referendum a vote among a group of people about a single issue

republic a country with an elected head of state and elected representatives

SEATO an anticommunist alliance made among Australia and several other Western and Asian countries; SEATO was dissolved in 1977

Southern Hemisphere the area of Earth south of the equator, the imaginary line that goes around the middle of the planet

sustainable capable of being maintained or repeated

tsunami a series of giant, fast-moving surges of water caused by an undersea earthquake, landslide, or volcanic eruption

Soviet Union a communist country that existed from 1922 to 1991, consisted of 15 member states, and rivaled the United States as a major world power

vocational having to do with education that trains a person for a particular job or career

WWOOF short for "Willing Workers on Organic Farms," a program in Australia that provides people with opportunities to work on organic farms

Further Information

BOOKS TO READ

Arnold, Caroline, and Arthur P. Arnold. *Uluru: Australia's Aboriginal Heart.* Clarion Books, 2003.

Darian-Smith, Kate. *Australia, Antarctica, and the Pacific* (Continents of the World). World Almanac Library, 2005.

Darlington, Robert. *Australia* (Nations of the World). Raintree Publishers, 2004)

Einfeld, Jann. *Life in the Australian Outback* (The Way People Live). Lucent Books, 2002.

Heinrichs, Ann. *Australia* (Enchantment of the World, Second Series). Children's Press, 2006.

Leppman, Elizabeth J. *Australia and the Pacific* (Modern World Cultures). Chelsea House, 2005.

Mason, Paul. *Sydney* (Global Cities). Chelsea House, 2007.

National Geographic Society, Arthur Meier Schlesinger, editor. *Australia: The Unique Continent* (Cultural and Geographical Exploration). Chelsea House, 2000.

North, Peter. *Australia* (Countries of the World). Gareth Steven, 2003.)

Steele, Philip. *Sydney* (Great Cities of the World). World Almanac Library, 2004.

Walker, Kathryn. *Melbourne* (Great Cities of the World). World Almanac Library, 2005.

USEFUL WEB SITES

Australia: Beyond the Fatal Shore
www.pbs.org/wnet/australia/

Australian Bureau of Statistics
www.abs.gov.au

Australian Museum Online
www.amonline.net.au/features/index.cfm

Australian Platypus Conservancy
www.platypus.asn.au/home.html

The Department of the Prime Minister and Cabinet
www.dpmc.gov.au

Tasmania Parks and Wildlife Service
www.parks.tas.gov.au/nature.html

Publisher's note to educators and parents: Our editors have carefully reviewed these Web sites to ensure that they are suitable for children. Many Web sites change frequently, however, and we cannot guarantee that a site's future contents will continue to meet our high standards of quality and educational value. Be advised that children should be closely supervised whenever they access the Internet.

Index

Page numbers in **bold** indicate pictures.

About the Author

Otto James divides his time between writing for books and Web sites and traveling. He writes mainly about travel, geography, and sports.

Otto's favorite places in Australia are the First Drop Café, in Sydney, and Airey's Inlet, along Victoria's Great Ocean Road.